Social Media Privacy & Digital Footprint

How to Protect Your Online Presence, Limit Tracking, and Control What the Internet Knows About You

By Joe Correa

Published by Live Stronger Faster

This book is for educational and informational purposes only. The author and publisher are not engaged in rendering legal, financial, or other professional advice. Readers should consult a qualified professional before making any financial decisions.

First Edition

Table of Contents

Introduction

In today's world, social media has evolved far beyond its original purpose. What began as a tool to connect with friends and share life's highlights has grown into a digital ecosystem where your every move, thought, photo, comment, and like can be monitored, analyzed, and stored—forever. Platforms like Facebook, Instagram, TikTok, LinkedIn, X (formerly Twitter), and Snapchat have become woven into the fabric of our daily lives. Yet few users truly understand what they're giving up in exchange for that convenience, entertainment, or fleeting validation.

Every time you log in, post, react, or scroll, you leave behind a data trail—what cybersecurity experts call your **digital footprint**. This footprint contains far more than just your name and profile photo. It includes metadata like your exact location, the device you're using, your contact list, browsing habits, emotional reactions, shopping preferences, and even voice or facial patterns in some cases. Most of this is collected quietly and without your active knowledge. And the truth is, once it's out there, it's very hard—if not impossible—to take back.

What's most concerning is that your digital footprint is not just used to "improve your user experience." It's sold, profiled, and manipulated—often to advertisers, political campaigns, and data brokers. Platforms use your behavior to predict what you'll do next, and algorithms are trained to show you content that keeps you engaged, even if it's polarizing or harmful. This invisible web of surveillance capitalism means that your online life is no longer just your business—it's *big* business.

This book is designed to give you back control. Whether you're a casual user sharing family updates, a business owner promoting your brand, a parent trying to protect your children, or someone trying to reduce their digital exposure, you'll learn how to limit what the internet knows about you and how to stop feeding an ecosystem that profits from your information. You'll discover practical, easy-to-follow steps to clean up your digital footprint, manage your account settings, prevent data leaks, and even reduce your online presence altogether if you choose.

But this isn't just about locking down your settings or deleting your old posts. It's about *understanding the system.* We'll uncover how social media platforms profile your behavior, how shadow accounts are created using your friends' and contacts' data, and how data brokers collect and resell your personal information. You'll learn what metadata really is—and why it matters. You'll also gain insight into how the next generation, including kids and teens, are uniquely vulnerable to privacy violations that can follow them for life.

At the same time, we'll explore how to be a mindful digital citizen in a world that encourages oversharing. We'll look at the psychological impact of social media, why digital detoxing matters, and how to create a relationship with these platforms that's based on intention rather than addiction. You'll learn how to separate your personal and professional lives online, use anonymity tools if needed, and avoid common pitfalls that can damage your reputation or even jeopardize your safety.

This book doesn't assume you're going to quit social media altogether. Most people can't—and many don't want to. That's why this guide isn't anti-technology. Instead, it's pro-*privacy*, pro-*agency*, and pro-*informed choice*. You don't need to disappear from the internet. You just need to become aware of what you're sharing, who you're sharing it with, and what they're doing with that information behind the scenes.

Social media isn't inherently evil. It's a tool. And like any tool, it can be used to build something great—or it can be used to destroy trust, privacy, and well-being. The goal is to help you understand how to use social media *on your own terms*. To empower you with knowledge so that you're not just a passive user in someone else's game, but an active participant in shaping your digital identity and protecting your personal boundaries.

Your digital life is yours. Let's make sure you're the one in control.

Chapter 1: The Digital Footprint You Didn't Know You Had

Most people don't realize they're leaving behind a trail every time they interact with the internet. This trail is called a **digital footprint**, and it's much more detailed and permanent than most users imagine. It's not just your posts or profile pictures–it's the invisible data created and collected from your online behaviors, whether you're logged in or not. Every time you click a link, like a comment, install an app, or use a map service, you're adding to this footprint.

There are two types of digital footprints: **active** and **passive**. An active footprint includes anything you intentionally publish or share, such as uploading a photo to Instagram or leaving a comment on a YouTube video. A passive footprint, on the other hand, is created without your knowledge. This includes data gathered from cookies, trackers, IP addresses, GPS signals, device IDs, and behavioral analytics. The moment you visit a website, scroll a page, or pause on a video–even without clicking–you're contributing to this passive footprint.

What's more alarming is that this data is often collected across multiple platforms, combined, and stored indefinitely. Social media companies, advertisers, and even third-party data brokers use tracking technologies to build complex profiles on users. These profiles are then sold, analyzed, and used to predict your behavior. They may know your age, income level, political views, mental health status, and even your sleep schedule—all inferred from digital behavior.

Most users assume that deleting a post or account means the data is gone. But that's far from the truth. Data backups, third-party access logs, cached content, and screenshots mean that content lives far beyond deletion. Even when you delete your data, platforms may retain it under vague "data retention" clauses in their privacy policies. Some data brokers gather information from public records, others scrape social platforms or purchase data from apps with loose privacy restrictions. The average user may be unaware of how many entities possess their personal data, or how it's being used.

This lack of visibility has serious consequences. Employers, colleges, landlords, and even dating matches often research people online. One offensive comment, embarrassing photo, or inaccurate tag from years ago can damage your reputation. In some countries, digital footprints can even influence your credit score or visa applications. And in the wrong hands, even simple data—like your email address or birthday—can be used to reset your accounts or commit identity theft.

The concept of a permanent, searchable archive of your digital life may sound like science fiction, but it's already here. Search engines like Google cache information long after it's deleted from the source. Facial recognition can link your social profiles even if you've changed your name. AI can identify people in group photos who never agreed to be tagged. And third-party advertisers can use data cross-matching to identify you with shocking accuracy.

Fortunately, there are ways to **minimize** your digital footprint. You can start by conducting a personal data audit: search your name, email address, and usernames on search engines. Check what's visible publicly. Remove old accounts or unused apps. Update privacy settings across all platforms. Use search engines and browsers that don't track you, such as DuckDuckGo or Brave. Disable location history and ad personalization wherever possible. Be selective about what you post, and assume that anything shared online may become public forever.

The most powerful defense is awareness. Understand that the internet is not a private place, even when platforms claim it is. Privacy settings can help, but they don't eliminate tracking. And remember, social media platforms are businesses—they exist to monetize your data. The more informed you are, the more intentional your digital choices become.

Your digital footprint is more than data—it's a reflection of your identity, habits, and values. By learning how it's formed and where it leads, you can take back control of your privacy and your future in the digital world.

Carla's social media story

It started with a Google search. Carla, a 27-year-old marketing assistant, was applying for a new job and wanted to make sure her online presence looked professional. She typed her name into the search bar, expecting to see only her LinkedIn profile and a few work-related mentions. What she found instead made her heart sink.

There were photos from college parties she didn't remember attending. A three-year-old tweet from a now-defunct account with a sarcastic joke taken out of context. A video where she was in the background at a protest—nothing illegal, but controversial enough to raise eyebrows. There was even an outdated Yelp review she'd written five years ago complaining about a local coffee shop. Somehow, it had all been indexed, stored, and surfaced. She felt exposed.

Curious and disturbed, Carla kept digging. She used a tool that showed what data brokers had on her. It included her full name, age, phone numbers, previous addresses, estimated income, political leanings, and even details about her shopping habits. She hadn't signed up for any of this. She hadn't given explicit consent. Yet here it was, all laid out, packaged, and sold to whoever wanted to buy it.

The deeper she looked, the more unsettled she became. Her smartphone had been tracking her location history for years. Apps she'd downloaded "just to try" were accessing her microphone and camera in the background. Her personal photos were being scanned for metadata, and facial recognition had quietly tagged her in group images uploaded by other people. Her digital life wasn't just public—it was *predictable.* And that predictability had value for marketers, political campaigns, and even hackers.

Carla remembered how freely she used to post online. She loved sharing travel photos, recipes, funny memes, and thoughts about current events. She thought deleting old content meant it was gone. She thought "private account" meant only friends could see it. But now, with fresh eyes, she realized that privacy online was mostly an illusion—especially on platforms designed to collect, not protect.

Determined to change things, Carla spent a weekend scrubbing her digital footprint. She deleted old social accounts, adjusted every privacy setting she could find, and requested data removal from several broker sites. She switched to a browser that didn't track her, turned off location history on her phone, and started using encrypted messaging apps. It didn't erase everything—but it helped.

Most importantly, it changed how she viewed the internet. She no longer posted impulsively. She thought twice about what she shared and with whom. She realized that her digital footprint wasn't just about reputation—it was about *control.* Control over her future, her identity, and how she wanted the world to see her.

Carla didn't stop using social media, but she stopped being a passive user. She understood that while she couldn't erase her past completely, she could start shaping her digital future with intention. That awareness became her shield.

In a world where data is currency and algorithms know you better than your friends do, Carla chose to reclaim her privacy—one step at a time.

Chapter 2: What Social Media Platforms Know About You

When you use social media, it's easy to believe that the only information you're sharing is what you manually type or upload. You post a photo, write a caption, comment on a friend's update, and move on. But behind the scenes, social media platforms are collecting a staggering amount of data — not just from what you say or share, but from *how* you use the platform, *when*, and *where*. The result? A detailed psychological and behavioral profile far more sophisticated than most people imagine.

Let's break it down. First, there's **profile data** — the most obvious and voluntary information you give away. This includes your name, birthday, email address, phone number, gender, interests, relationships, and job title. Many platforms also ask for optional information, like your education, previous work, cities you've lived in, and even religious and political views. While you may skip some of these fields, every detail you enter trains the platform's algorithm to better understand you — and monetize your activity.

Beyond what you give voluntarily is **behavioral data** — and this is where things get more invasive. Platforms track how long you spend on posts, which videos you watch to the end, what topics you pause on, what time of day you're most active, how often you message certain people, and how quickly you scroll. Even if you don't click "like" or leave a comment, your hesitation or interest is logged. These subtle behaviors help platforms gauge your preferences and tailor your feed for maximum engagement — and maximum profit.

They also collect **technical and device data**. This includes your device ID, operating system, browser type, screen resolution, battery level, storage usage, and Bluetooth or Wi-Fi network connections. Your IP address provides geolocation data, and your microphone and camera — when permissions are enabled — may be accessed to capture ambient sound and video behavior. Some apps even request access to your contact list, syncing phone numbers and email addresses of people you know, even if they're not on the platform.

What about your messages? While most platforms claim to protect your private messages, metadata is still collected. This includes who you messaged, when, how often, and for how long. If you're using a platform that scans messages for content moderation or ad targeting (as many do), the contents themselves may be processed — especially if they're stored on company servers.

Social media companies also engage in **off-platform tracking**. This means they monitor your behavior on other websites and apps, even when you're not using their service. This is done through cookies, tracking pixels, social share buttons, and integrations with partner sites. Ever noticed how you search for a product on one website, and ads for that product immediately appear on Instagram? That's no coincidence — that's integrated data sharing in action.

Moreover, your activity contributes to what's known as a **shadow profile**. This is a data profile built on you, even if you never signed up for the platform. If your friends grant contact access, upload group photos, or tag you in content, the platform can use that data to connect the dots. The more people you interact with, the more accurate your shadow profile becomes — without you ever touching the app.

Another layer is **emotional and psychological analysis**. Platforms use AI to interpret sentiment from your posts, comments, emojis, and reactions. They can identify whether you're happy, sad, angry, anxious, or celebratory. Combined with timing, this can be used to predict behavior, such as shopping habits, voting tendencies, or even signs of mental health issues. Some platforms have been criticized for using this data to target vulnerable users or influence emotions during product launches or elections.

All of this information is collected under the guise of "personalization." But the true goal is optimization – optimizing for ad revenue, content virality, and behavioral prediction. Your data fuels an ecosystem where attention is currency, and manipulation is science.

The good news is you can fight back. Start by reviewing your permissions – remove access to contacts, location, and unnecessary device features. Disable ad personalization and interest-based tracking. Turn off face recognition and voice activity logging. Avoid linking your social media accounts to other apps, and resist logging in with "Sign in with Facebook" or "Sign in with Google."

Next, use your platform's "Download My Data" or "Access Your Information" tools. These can reveal just how much data has been stored about you. Finally, adopt privacy-first habits: use burner emails for signups, avoid sharing personal milestones publicly, and check your account activity logs regularly.

Understanding what social media knows about you isn't about paranoia – it's about empowerment. The more you know, the more you can choose how much of yourself you allow the digital world to access and influence.

Diego's suspicious social media ad

Diego had always considered himself tech-savvy. As a freelance graphic designer, he used social media to promote his work, stay inspired, and connect with potential clients. He had profiles on Instagram, LinkedIn, Facebook, and TikTok. He carefully curated his content, posted regularly, and engaged with his followers. But he never imagined that the platforms he trusted to grow his business were quietly building a dossier on him — one that went far deeper than he ever approved.

It started when Diego received a strange ad on Instagram — a product he had only talked about out loud in his apartment, never typed, searched, or shared. It felt uncanny, like his phone had eavesdropped on a private conversation. Curious and a bit creeped out, he decided to dig into his account settings.

He found that his Instagram app had microphone access enabled, along with location tracking "only while using the app" — which in practice meant nearly all the time. His Facebook settings showed that his contact list had been synced automatically, and the app had collected his call history and text message logs for "improving suggestions." Diego hadn't even realized that was possible. Worse, he discovered an activity log that showed how long he'd viewed specific posts, what he'd clicked on, and even items he looked at but didn't like.

When he downloaded his full Facebook data archive, he was shocked to find over 1,000 pages of personal information – including old conversations, location history, ad interactions, political interest tags, and even facial recognition data from photos he never uploaded himself. The platform had created a map of his digital life, including information he thought was private or forgotten.

The kicker was discovering that Facebook had been tracking his activity *outside* of the platform – which websites he visited, what time he opened apps, and what purchases he made through affiliate partners. A trail of behavior had been pieced together, forming a version of Diego he barely recognized: one optimized for targeted advertising and algorithmic influence.

He felt betrayed, not because he didn't know some data was being collected, but because the scope was far greater than what had been communicated. The platform hadn't just observed his behavior – it had predicted and manipulated it. He began to question how much of his feed was truly organic, and how much had been shaped by machine-learning models designed to keep him engaged.

Determined to regain control, Diego took action. He revoked app permissions, turned off microphone and location access, and disconnected his social accounts from third-party apps. He stopped logging in through Google and started using encrypted browsers and private search engines. He also began posting less frequently and avoided sharing personal milestones. Most importantly, he became more intentional with his scrolling — not letting the algorithm dictate his attention.

Diego didn't delete his accounts. He still needed them for business, but he now treated them like tools — not companions. He realized that the platforms knew more about him than some of his closest friends. But unlike his friends, they weren't listening to help him — they were listening to *sell* him.

His perspective shifted. He no longer assumed privacy by default. He understood that in the digital economy, data is currency — and he'd been spending it carelessly. From that point on, Diego approached every app, every click, and every post with a single thought: *What are they learning about me right now — and why?*

And with that awareness, he began to draw the line between connection and control.

Chapter 3: How to Lock Down Your Accounts

Securing your social media accounts is one of the most effective ways to protect your digital privacy and reduce the risk of being hacked, tracked, or impersonated. Most people assume that simply using a password and adjusting a few privacy settings is enough—but in today's digital environment, that's no longer sufficient. Social media platforms are powerful data collection tools, and without the right configurations, they can expose more about you than you ever intended. This chapter will walk you through exactly how to "lock down" your accounts across the most popular platforms so you can regain control of your digital presence.

Start with your **passwords**. Never reuse the same password across multiple sites. If one account is breached, it could create a domino effect. Use a password manager to generate and store long, complex passwords—ideally 16 characters or more with a mix of uppercase, lowercase, numbers, and special characters. Avoid anything related to your birthday, pet's name, or favorite sports team. If a platform offers **two-factor authentication (2FA)** or **multi-factor authentication (MFA)**, enable it immediately. This adds an extra layer of security by requiring a code from your phone or authentication app in addition to your password.

Next, review your **privacy and security settings** platform by platform. On **Facebook**, go to the Privacy Checkup tool. Turn off face recognition, disable search engine indexing, and limit who can find you by email or phone number. Restrict who can see your friends list and past posts. On **Instagram**, set your account to private if you're not using it professionally. Disable message requests from people you don't follow. On **TikTok**, go to Privacy Settings to block downloads of your videos and turn off ad personalization. On **LinkedIn**, hide your connections, disable profile viewing history, and opt out of data sharing with third parties. On **Twitter/X**, set your tweets to private if needed, disable location tagging, and restrict direct messages to people you follow.

Also, review which **apps and devices are connected** to your accounts. Over time, we grant access to dozens of third-party apps—quiz games, email finders, analytics tools—that continue collecting data long after we stop using them. Revoke access to anything unfamiliar or unused. Check your login activity and remove old sessions from devices you no longer use. This is especially important if you've ever used a shared or public computer to access your account.

Turn off or limit **location tracking**. Platforms often embed

GPS metadata in your content without you realizing it. Even if you don't tag your location in a post, your device might be doing it automatically. Disable location sharing in your phone settings, and avoid posting while you're still at a physical location—especially home, work, or frequent hangouts.

Next, manage your **tagging and visibility**. Set your profile so that posts you're tagged in require your approval before appearing publicly. This prevents friends or followers from associating you with content that could hurt your reputation. You should also hide your birthday, relationship status, and other personal details that identity thieves or social engineers often target.

Don't forget about **profile pictures and bios**. Even if your account is private, these elements are usually visible to everyone. Avoid using photos that reveal your exact location (e.g., house address, school name, license plate). Use a general or professional description in your bio, and don't include personal contact information unless necessary.

Finally, conduct a **quarterly digital audit**. Search your name on major search engines and see what comes up. Review your settings to ensure nothing changed during app updates. Platforms often alter privacy options without alerting users, resetting certain permissions or introducing new defaults that are less secure. Stay informed by following tech blogs or privacy advocacy sites that track these updates.

By implementing these steps across your social media profiles, you significantly reduce the risk of unauthorized access, data harvesting, and exposure. You don't need to disappear from the internet—you just need to be smarter about how you show up.

The goal isn't to hide—it's to protect your time, identity, and peace of mind. Your accounts should work *for* you, not against you. Take the time to lock them down now—and sleep easier knowing you're in control.

Now, lets do over Asha's story

Asha loved social media. As a small business owner, she used it to promote her handmade candles and connect with customers across the country. Her Instagram was beautifully curated, her Facebook page was active with reviews, and her TikTok videos often went viral. But everything changed the day she woke up to dozens of messages from friends saying they had received strange messages from her. Some had even clicked suspicious links she'd supposedly sent.

She was locked out of her accounts. Someone had taken control of her profiles overnight.

Panicked, Asha tried to reset her passwords, but the hacker had already changed the email and phone number associated with her login. Worse, they'd begun posting spammy ads to her followers and sending malicious links in her name. Her brand reputation—built over three years—was unraveling in real-time.

With the help of a tech-savvy friend, Asha eventually regained access to her accounts. But the experience left her shaken. She realized she had never taken her online security seriously. Her passwords were variations of her dog's name. She had reused them across multiple platforms. She had never enabled two-factor authentication. And she had no idea how many third-party apps had access to her profiles.

Determined not to let it happen again, Asha began locking down every account she owned. She installed a password manager and created strong, unique passwords. She turned on two-factor authentication for everything—from her email to her social platforms to her online store. She revoked access to over 20 connected apps she didn't even remember authorizing.

Then she dove into her privacy settings. On Facebook, she limited who could see her posts, removed her birthday and location, and disabled the ability for others to tag her without approval. She removed herself from public search engines. On

Instagram, she reviewed every story highlight and archived old posts that showed too much personal detail. On TikTok, she blocked downloads of her content and disabled ad personalization. She even updated her LinkedIn to hide her connections list and turned off email syncing.

Asha also deleted old devices from her login history and started logging out when she wasn't using her accounts. She stopped using public Wi-Fi for anything sensitive and began using a virtual private network (VPN) while working in cafés. What surprised her most wasn't how hard the process was—it was how *easy* it had been to overlook these simple steps for so long.

Months later, Asha's business was thriving again. But this time, she had peace of mind. She no longer feared waking up to chaos. Her confidence wasn't just in her brand—it was in the knowledge that she had done the work to protect it.

She began teaching other small business owners about digital security at local workshops. She shared her story, her checklist, and her lessons. And every time she did, she reminded them of the same truth she had learned the hard way:

"Your social media account is not just a profile—it's your reputation, your business, and your identity. Protect it like your future depends on it—because it just might."

Chapter 4: Reduce, Remove, and Reclaim Control

Every time you share something online—whether it's a photo, comment, check-in, or like—it contributes to your digital presence. Over time, these actions build a massive, often uncontrollable archive of your life. The goal of this chapter is simple: help you reduce that digital clutter, remove unnecessary or risky data, and reclaim control of what the world—and algorithms—know about you.

The first step is conducting a **personal data audit**. Start by Googling yourself. Use different variations of your name, usernames, email addresses, and even phone numbers. See what appears on the first few pages of results, including images, comments, and past posts. Do this in an incognito browser to see what an outsider would find. Note anything you'd like to remove or hide.

Next, log in to each of your social media platforms and review your **timeline or activity history**. Facebook, for example, has an Activity Log that allows you to review everything you've posted, liked, or been tagged in. Instagram provides an "Your Activity" dashboard where you can manage interactions and archived content. TikTok and X (formerly Twitter) also allow access to past activity—though sometimes buried under layers of settings.

Start **deleting old content** that no longer serves you. Remove embarrassing posts, irrelevant opinions, personal location check-ins, or anything that could be taken out of context. Delete comments you regret. Remove tagged photos that don't align with your current image or values. And remember, just because something was once okay to share doesn't mean it still is today.

Then, download your **full data archive** from each platform. Most sites now offer this feature in compliance with privacy laws like GDPR and CCPA. On Facebook, go to "Settings > Your Facebook Information > Download Your Information." On Instagram, navigate to "Settings > Your Activity > Download Your Information." The downloaded files will show what data is stored about you—including things you may have forgotten or never knew were collected.

Now it's time to address **third-party platforms**. Your digital footprint isn't just on social media—it's scattered across comment sections, blogs, forums, shopping sites, and data broker databases. Use tools like **JustDeleteMe**, **DeleteMe**, or **PrivacyBee** to remove your data from hundreds of sites that aggregate your information and sell it. You can also manually request removal from websites using opt-out links or emails found in their privacy policies.

To prevent new data from accumulating, **adjust your habits** moving forward. Avoid using real names on public forums. Don't grant unnecessary permissions when installing new apps. Say no to syncing contacts or allowing location access unless absolutely necessary. Log out of services when not in use, and disable cross-platform tracking whenever possible.

Set a recurring schedule—perhaps once a quarter—to **revisit and clean up your digital presence**. Think of it like spring cleaning for your online life. Regularly reviewing your accounts, clearing search history, and deleting unused profiles ensures you stay in control.

Also, consider using **alias accounts or email addresses** for non-essential signups. This prevents your primary identity from being tied to dozens of third-party services. If you want to interact with certain communities but remain anonymous, use a pseudonym and limit personal sharing.

Keep in mind that once something is shared online, you may not be able to fully erase it. Screenshots, cached content, and data backups mean that some posts live on—even after deletion. But reducing your visible footprint and tightening control over future content is still a powerful step toward digital privacy.

The goal isn't to erase your existence online. It's to be **intentional and strategic** about what you share, where you share it, and who gets to see it. Your digital presence should reflect the person you are today—not the person you were ten years ago. And it should never be shaped by someone else's business model.

Now, I want to talk about Marcus.

Marcus never really thought about his digital footprint. Like most people, he used social media without giving much thought to the trail he was leaving behind. He'd been on Facebook since high school, joined Twitter during college, and picked up Instagram along the way. Over the years, his accounts became a museum of forgotten jokes, party photos, political rants, and casual oversharing. It wasn't until he applied for a job at a tech company that he realized just how exposed he was.

During the interview process, Marcus overheard one of the hiring managers mention a "background review." They weren't just talking about criminal checks—they were Googling candidates and scanning social media. That night, Marcus searched his name online. What he saw shocked him.

There were photos of him from college wearing a costume he now regretted. Tweets from 2014 that made him cringe. Posts ranting about past employers. He even found a long-forgotten Tumblr blog where he'd written angsty poetry as a teenager—now indexed by Google for the world to see. Even worse, he discovered his full address listed on a data broker site, along with his phone number and estimated income.

That night, Marcus barely slept. By morning, he was on a mission.

He started by cleaning house. On Facebook, he went through his activity log and deleted hundreds of old posts. He removed his birthday, education history, and hometown. He untagged himself from dozens of photos, then messaged friends asking them to remove others. On Twitter, he deleted old tweets with a bulk-removal tool and protected his future posts. He locked down his Instagram and archived everything that didn't fit the image he wanted to present now.

Then he moved beyond social media. He requested removal from data broker sites. He used a service that helped him opt out of people-search websites. He deleted accounts from forums and shopping sites he no longer used. He even contacted an old blog host to request that his abandoned blog be taken offline.

Marcus didn't stop there. He changed how he interacted online altogether. He created a separate email account for signing up for new services and avoided giving his real name when it wasn't necessary. He stopped tagging his location in real time and disabled ad personalization across platforms. He even set quarterly calendar reminders to audit his digital presence—just like checking in on his credit report or finances.

The transformation was liberating. Marcus felt like he'd taken back control over his identity. He wasn't ashamed of his past, but he didn't want it to define his future—or be twisted out of context by strangers. His job application wasn't derailed, and eventually, he landed a position at a company that valued privacy and digital awareness.

What surprised Marcus most was how little effort it took to make such a big difference. Most of the work could be done in a few hours—but the peace of mind it gave him was lasting. He felt safer. Smarter. More intentional. He even began speaking at local tech meetups, sharing his story and encouraging others to reclaim their digital footprint.

For Marcus, the internet hadn't changed—but how he used it had. He no longer treated social media like a diary or a megaphone. He saw it for what it was: a powerful tool that, if left unchecked, could become a liability. But in the right hands, it could also be a platform for growth, connection, and control.

And this time, those hands were his.

Chapter 5: The Invisible Web – Metadata and Shadow Profiles

When we think about online data, we usually imagine names, addresses, photos, or typed-out posts. But the reality is that some of the most powerful—and intrusive—data online is **invisible to the user**. This hidden layer is called **metadata**, and it plays a critical role in how platforms, advertisers, and even governments track, profile, and predict human behavior. In parallel, social platforms also build **shadow profiles**—collections of data on people who haven't even signed up for their services. Understanding both metadata and shadow profiles is key to managing your digital footprint.

Metadata is often described as "data about data." It doesn't include the actual content of your message or post, but instead describes the context around it. For example, when you take a photo on your phone, the photo's metadata can include the time it was taken, your exact GPS location, the type of phone you used, and the file format. When you send an email, metadata includes the sender, recipient, timestamp, device used, and even your IP address. When you visit a website, metadata may include how long you stayed, where you clicked, what device you were on, and which browser you used.

Social media platforms collect metadata every time you scroll, pause, swipe, post, message, or even hover over content. This data helps them understand your habits, preferences, and vulnerabilities. For example, lingering on posts about anxiety or heartbreak might signal emotional distress, prompting targeted ads for therapy apps or self-help books. Metadata can also be used for surveillance or automated decision-making by corporations and governments alike.

Many users mistakenly believe that turning off location services or going private will shield them from tracking. While these are good steps, they don't eliminate metadata collection. Most metadata is automatically generated and recorded behind the scenes, regardless of your privacy settings. Some platforms even strip away privacy protections when you upload content, allowing them to store metadata on their servers—indefinitely.

Now let's look at **shadow profiles**. These are digital dossiers built on people who have not explicitly created an account on a platform. Let's say your friend signs up for Facebook and grants access to their contacts. If your name, phone number, or email is in their contact list, Facebook can start building a shadow profile on you—even if you've never joined. The same thing happens when people tag you in photos or mention your name in posts.

Shadow profiles are controversial because they extend data collection beyond consent. They also allow platforms to track non-users and combine data across multiple sources. For instance, Facebook may know you visited a restaurant's website, even if you never use Facebook, thanks to embedded tracking pixels. Shadow profiles are rarely disclosed to the public, and users cannot view or delete the data they contain—making them a serious privacy concern.

Another issue is how metadata and shadow profile data are used to **train algorithms**. This includes facial recognition systems, targeted advertising, content recommendations, and even political influence campaigns. In the wrong hands, metadata can identify your routines, track your movements, or determine your relationships based on communication frequency or mutual connections.

To minimize your exposure to metadata tracking and shadow profiles, take proactive steps:

- **Strip metadata** from files before uploading. You can use tools to remove GPS data from photos or anonymize PDF files.

- **Use encrypted apps** like Signal or ProtonMail for communication—these tools minimize metadata retention.

- **Avoid granting access** to your contacts, photos, microphone, and location unless absolutely necessary.
- **Log out** of platforms when not in use to prevent cross-site tracking.
- **Use privacy-first browsers** and plugins like uBlock Origin or Privacy Badger to block trackers and fingerprinting scripts.
- **Educate your friends and family** about the risks of contact syncing—your privacy depends partly on their decisions too.

While you can't eliminate all metadata or avoid shadow profiling completely, awareness and action will dramatically reduce your exposure. Remember: what you *don't see* is often what matters most. In the digital world, invisible data can have *very real* consequences.

Leah's shadow profile story

Leah considered herself a cautious internet user. She kept her Instagram private, never shared her location, and avoided posting too much about her personal life. But one day, her younger brother Max made an offhand comment that left her unsettled. "That photo you sent Mom? I saw it on Facebook yesterday," he said. But Leah had never posted that photo—she had only texted it to her mother directly.

Curious and concerned, Leah started digging. She discovered that her mom had auto-synced her phone's photo gallery to Facebook. Without realizing it, her mother's account had uploaded the image to a private album that was still searchable through Facebook's algorithm. That's when Leah began to understand the power of **metadata**—and how easily it could be used to track her, even without her involvement.

Leah began researching the concept of metadata. She learned that every photo she took was stamped with information: the date, time, device model, and precise GPS coordinates. She had hundreds of photos sitting in cloud storage with metadata that revealed where she lived, worked, exercised, and vacationed—data that could be accessed or scraped under the right conditions.

She checked her email metadata next. Even the emails she thought were private contained headers showing her IP address and device information. A simple email to a friend could reveal her rough location or when she was online. Then she realized that the messaging apps she used every day tracked when she was active, when she was typing, who she contacted most often, and how long her conversations lasted.

But what shocked Leah most was learning about **shadow profiles**. She had never created a Facebook account, yet she found out through a friend's contact syncing that Facebook likely had her name, number, and email on file. When she tried to search for her own name, Facebook even suggested creating an account—complete with pre-filled suggestions of people she might know. It was as if she had been part of the network all along.

The feeling of being tracked without consent made her uneasy. She hadn't opted into this ecosystem, yet it had found its way into her life through the people around her. Her digital presence extended far beyond what she had posted herself. It was a reminder that privacy wasn't just personal—it was collective.

Determined to regain control, Leah began her cleanup. She downloaded a tool to scrub metadata from her photos. She switched to a privacy-focused browser and installed anti-tracking plugins. She stopped using apps that required contact syncing and asked her friends to do the same. She even reached out to her mom to help her disable automatic photo uploads.

Leah also started using encrypted messaging apps for conversations with her closest circle. She felt relieved knowing her chats weren't being stored in a database or scanned for ad purposes. Every change she made gave her more peace of mind, more control, and more confidence that she wasn't blindly surrendering her digital identity.

It wasn't about hiding–it was about choice. Leah realized that data collection wasn't evil by default, but it became dangerous when it was invisible, involuntary, and unaccountable. She decided she would no longer live in the shadow of a profile she didn't create.

From that day forward, Leah treated her metadata with the same respect she gave her passwords, photos, and finances. It was part of who she was–so it deserved to be protected.

Chapter 6: AI, Algorithms, and Manipulation

Social media platforms are not just passive websites where you post updates and connect with friends. Behind the scenes, they are powered by **AI-driven algorithms** designed to shape your behavior, guide your attention, and subtly influence what you believe and how you feel. While these algorithms are often framed as tools for "personalizing your experience," they are, in reality, **manipulation engines** optimized for maximum engagement and profit.

Every time you interact with content—whether by clicking, scrolling, pausing, liking, commenting, or sharing—you're training the algorithm. Artificial intelligence uses that data to learn what grabs your attention, what emotions you respond to, and what keeps you on the platform longer. Over time, your feed stops reflecting the broader world and instead becomes an echo chamber designed to confirm your biases, fuel your emotions, and keep you clicking.

This phenomenon is called a **filter bubble**, and it happens when the algorithm shows you more of what you already believe or like, while filtering out differing viewpoints. While it might feel comfortable, it's dangerous. You may begin to lose touch with reality, believe distorted versions of events, or develop extreme views based on repetitive exposure to a narrow set of content. Many political, cultural, and public health debates have been heavily distorted by algorithmic manipulation—often without users realizing it.

But it's not just news that's affected. **Product recommendations, friend suggestions, ads, and even dating matches** are curated using AI. These systems don't just observe your behavior—they predict your future decisions. The algorithm learns that if you're sad late at night, you're more likely to make impulse purchases. If you've been watching breakup videos, you might soon see ads for self-help books or even alcohol delivery services. Your emotions become a *product*.

Worse still, **algorithms can amplify misinformation and outrage**. Posts that make people angry or afraid tend to get more reactions, shares, and comments. The AI doesn't understand truth or context—it understands virality. This creates a feedback loop where false, divisive, or extreme content gets promoted over thoughtful, nuanced information. Studies show that users exposed to algorithmic news feeds are more likely to adopt polarized beliefs—even when they think they're making independent choices.

Another layer of concern is **manipulation through**

microtargeting. Advertisers can use behavioral data to deliver hyper-specific messages to you—messages no one else sees. This has been used to influence elections, suppress votes, or push vulnerable users toward predatory products. Because these messages are so targeted, there's little public accountability. You don't even know you're being manipulated—because it feels like a natural part of your feed.

So, what can you do to **regain control**?

First, **become aware of how the algorithm works**. Ask yourself why you're seeing a particular post or ad. Platforms like Instagram and Facebook now offer explanations like "You're seeing this because..." in their ad settings—check them often. Use this to adjust your preferences and block irrelevant or manipulative content.

Second, **follow a wide variety of sources** to break out of your bubble. Intentionally engage with different viewpoints, and don't rely on social media as your only source of news. Use independent news apps or visit websites directly.

Third, **limit emotional triggers**. Avoid engaging with content that makes you feel angry or overly reactive. The algorithm learns from your emotional intensity. If you react strongly, it will feed you more of the same. Instead, pause and reflect before liking, commenting, or sharing.

Fourth, **use manual browsing and curation**. Instead of endlessly scrolling a feed, go directly to creators or accounts you trust. Create saved lists or folders to organize your information and avoid algorithmic suggestions entirely.

Finally, consider **taking breaks**. Social media platforms are designed to be addictive. The infinite scroll, the likes, and the notifications are all dopamine triggers. Stepping away helps you reset your perspective and reduce your exposure to manipulation.

The truth is, artificial intelligence isn't neutral—it has been trained to maximize attention and revenue, not truth or well-being. But when you understand the system, you can step outside of it. You can use these platforms as tools, rather than letting them use you as a target.

Control starts with awareness—and awareness starts right here.

How Jamal learned to manage social media

Jamal loved late-night scrolling. It had become a habit—finish work, make a snack, and dive into his feed to unwind. TikTok, YouTube, and Instagram were his favorites. He'd laugh at memes, watch a few videos about sneakers or gaming, and check what his friends were up to. But over time, something started to change.

His feed shifted. The jokes became darker. The videos more aggressive. He started seeing conspiracy theories, angry rants, and "truth bombs" about politics, dating, and society. At first, it was entertaining. Then it became addictive. He'd stay up hours later than planned, falling into emotional rabbit holes. He felt outraged, then confused, then strangely energized. But he couldn't stop.

One day, Jamal snapped out of it. He was watching a video that claimed something wild about world events—something he knew wasn't true. But the comments were filled with agreement. When he googled it, he found the actual story was completely different. It was a wake-up call.

He began to question everything. Why was this the content being shown to him? Who decided this was what he needed to see? That night, he clicked into his account settings and discovered something that stunned him. His "ad interests" profile had him pegged as anxious, emotional, politically reactive, and impulsive. His watch time showed that he lingered longer on content that stirred fear or anger. The algorithm had simply followed the breadcrumbs—and fed him more of what kept him hooked.

Jamal felt manipulated. The feed hadn't just reflected his interests—it had *shaped* them. It had quietly nudged him into spending more time on the platform by fueling his worst emotions. He realized the system wasn't built for his benefit—it was built to profit from his attention.

Determined to take back control, Jamal unfollowed dozens of toxic accounts and started curating his feed more carefully. He added educational creators, mental health resources, and positive voices. He began visiting trusted news websites instead of relying on algorithmic recommendations. He installed screen time limits and muted notifications that used to keep him checking the app every few minutes.

But most importantly, Jamal changed his mindset. He stopped accepting his feed as a neutral reflection of reality. He asked questions: *Why is this going viral? What emotion is this trying to trigger? Who profits from my reaction?*

Slowly, the fog lifted. He felt more focused. More grounded. Less reactive. The content changed too—once he stopped feeding the algorithm with outrage, it stopped serving it back.

Jamal still used social media, but now *on his own terms.* No more doom-scrolling. No more emotional traps. No more invisible strings pulling at his mind. He finally understood that when you give an algorithm the steering wheel, it will drive you toward whatever keeps you on the platform—not necessarily what's good for you.

But when you grab that wheel back, you're not just scrolling. You're choosing.

Chapter 7: Kids, Teens, and the Risk of Oversharing

Children and teenagers are growing up in a world where digital sharing is not optional—it's expected. From birth announcements to birthday livestreams, from TikTok dances to school selfies, today's youth are raised in the public eye of social media. While these platforms may seem harmless—or even fun—the truth is that **oversharing** among children, teens, and even their parents poses significant and lasting privacy risks.

Let's start with **"sharenting."** This term refers to parents who frequently post photos, videos, and personal updates about their children online. While intentions may be innocent—documenting growth or sharing joyful moments—these posts can lead to unintended consequences. Photos of children are often uploaded with full names, birth dates, school names, and even geotags revealing their location. This information becomes part of a child's permanent digital footprint *before* they even understand what privacy is.

Oversharing can make children vulnerable to **identity theft, stalking, facial recognition tracking, and even deepfake abuse** later in life. Some parents accidentally post images that include medical records, home addresses, or other identifiers. Worse, children cannot consent to their online image being shared, yet it becomes searchable and sometimes copied without permission.

For teens who manage their own accounts, the stakes are even higher. Adolescents often lack the maturity to evaluate the **long-term impact** of what they post. A video made on impulse, a post shared during emotional stress, or a comment made in jest can go viral—or be screenshotted and saved for future blackmail, bullying, or reputation damage. What's meant to be temporary may live forever.

Moreover, social media use among youth contributes to **mental health challenges**. Studies link excessive screen time and social comparison to higher rates of anxiety, depression, body image issues, and cyberbullying. Teens often chase validation through likes, followers, or comments, not realizing they are entering a system designed to be addictive and performative.

Another concern is **data profiling**. Platforms like TikTok, Snapchat, and Instagram collect behavioral data from teens just as aggressively as they do from adults. They track what content is watched, how long it's viewed, who is followed, which filters are used, and even biometric information like facial movements. This data is used to create psychological profiles, which may be used to push targeted ads or even content that encourages risky behavior.

So what can be done?

Parents and guardians must take a proactive role. First, set privacy rules for your own content. Avoid posting your child's full name, school, daily routine, or real-time location. Don't post photos of children in swimsuits, bathrooms, or private moments. Use nickname initials or emojis to conceal faces if needed. Ask yourself: "Would I want this photo of me online forever?"

Next, **talk to your children early and often** about digital boundaries. Teach them that the internet is permanent, that every post can be saved, and that privacy is a right worth protecting. Encourage them to think twice before posting. Help them adjust their account settings to private, and ensure they understand how to report or block harmful users.

For teens, set healthy screen time limits, but more importantly, build *awareness*. Discuss peer pressure, social media trends, and the dangers of oversharing. Instead of simply saying "don't do this," show them real-world consequences and help them make informed choices. Model healthy behavior yourself—because kids imitate adults more than they obey rules.

Use **parental controls and monitoring tools** like Apple Screen Time, Google Family Link, or third-party apps to stay aware of what platforms your child is using. But remember, monitoring is not the same as trust. Build an open dialogue so your child feels safe asking questions and sharing concerns.

Finally, consider establishing a **"digital contract"** with your child—a mutual agreement outlining responsibilities, limits, and expectations for internet use. Include rules for posting, interacting, and handling mistakes. Make it clear that online mistakes are forgivable, but honesty and awareness matter.

By teaching young people to value their privacy early, we empower them to become responsible digital citizens who use technology with confidence and control. The internet isn't going away. But with education, boundaries, and guidance, oversharing doesn't have to define their future.

Now, let's go over Emma's story

Emma was a proud mom. Her daughter Lily had just turned seven, and the birthday party had been magical—balloons, cake, and lots of laughter. Like many parents, Emma posted a few photos to Facebook: Lily blowing out candles, opening presents, and hugging her friends. She tagged the location, added a few hashtags, and watched as the likes and heart emojis poured in.

She didn't think much about it until her friend Sarah commented, "So cute! Same school as my nephew—small world!" That's when it hit Emma: she had posted Lily's full name, school uniform, and exact location in one photo. Anyone could see where her daughter went to school—and maybe even when she was there.

Emma's stomach turned. She thought her account was private, but upon double-checking, she realized her birthday album had been marked "Public." She began scrolling through her timeline and saw dozens of photos from the past few years—bath time, doctor's visits, beach vacations. All were sweet memories, but now they felt uncomfortably revealing.

Across town, 14-year-old Lucas was dealing with his own version of oversharing. He had just started high school and had a decent following on TikTok. One night, frustrated with a classmate, he posted a sarcastic video mocking a situation at school. It wasn't meant to be mean—but it mentioned a teacher by name. The video got more views than anything he'd posted before.

The next morning, Lucas was called into the principal's office. Someone had sent the video to school staff. The teacher was upset, and Lucas's parents were furious. He hadn't realized how quickly content could spread—or how serious the consequences could be. "I thought it would just stay on my page," he mumbled. "I didn't think anyone would care."

That night, Lucas deleted most of his past videos. He read through comments on old posts and realized how much personal information he had shared without noticing—his school name, his daily routine, even his bus stop. He felt exposed.

Both Emma and Lucas had learned the same lesson, just from different angles: the internet doesn't forget. What seems harmless in the moment can become a safety risk, a reputation issue, or a source of regret down the road.

Emma took action. She cleaned up her Facebook, removed photo tags, and stopped posting Lily's full face online. She started using private sharing apps for family updates. She also sat down with Lily and began teaching her about privacy—what it means, why it matters, and how to protect it. "Even though you're young," she told her, "you have the right to decide what the world sees."

Lucas, too, began changing his habits. He set his account to private and removed followers he didn't know personally. He started asking himself, "Would I be okay with my teacher—or my future boss—seeing this?" before posting. He still made funny videos, but now they focused on relatable topics, not real people or places.

Their stories weren't about fear—they were about growth. They realized that digital awareness isn't just for tech experts. It's for every parent, every teen, every kid holding a smartphone. It's about protecting the right to grow up without a permanent digital record of every mistake, joke, or photo.

Oversharing doesn't begin with bad intentions—but it often ends with unintended consequences. Fortunately, awareness can turn things around. Emma and Lucas learned that lesson in time—and so can others.

Chapter 8: Digital Detox and Mindful Social Media Use

The internet was designed to connect us, inform us, and entertain us—but somewhere along the way, it became overwhelming. Notifications never stop. Feeds never end. Messages pile up. And the line between real life and screen life becomes increasingly blurry. That's why **digital detoxing** and practicing **mindful social media use** are no longer luxuries—they're essential for mental clarity, emotional health, and regaining control over your time and energy.

Let's start with the problem: **social media is engineered to be addictive**. Every feature—the infinite scroll, the likes, the hearts, the pop-up notifications—is designed to trigger dopamine responses in the brain. These features create a feedback loop that keeps you coming back, often without conscious thought. The average person taps their phone over 2,600 times per day. Many of us start and end our days with screens, never giving our minds a true break.

The consequences are significant. Studies have shown links between excessive social media use and **anxiety, depression, poor sleep, low self-esteem, attention problems, and even loneliness**. Constant exposure to filtered perfection and performative happiness can warp your self-perception. Notifications hijack your attention and scatter your focus. And the pressure to stay "caught up" leaves many people feeling perpetually behind.

This is where **digital detoxing** comes in. A digital detox is not about deleting everything and going off the grid (unless you want to). It's about **creating intentional space** between you and your devices. It's about breaking unconscious patterns and retraining your brain to use technology as a tool, not a master.

Start with a **time audit**. Use screen time tracking apps like Moment, RescueTime, or Apple Screen Time to see how many hours you spend on social platforms. You may be surprised. Then, identify which apps or platforms drain your time without offering value. These are the ones to reduce or pause.

Next, set **"no phone" zones or times.** For example: no phones in bed, during meals, or the first hour after waking. Silence unnecessary notifications and remove social apps from your home screen. Use grayscale mode to make apps less visually enticing. Even simple changes like keeping your phone out of reach while working can drastically reduce compulsive checking.

Consider scheduling **"social media sabbaths."** Take one day a week off completely. Or try a weekend with no social apps. During this time, notice how you feel—do you miss it, or do you feel more focused, relaxed, and grounded?

When you do use social media, practice **mindful engagement**. Ask yourself: Why am I opening this app? What am I hoping to get out of it? Am I using it intentionally, or just reacting to boredom or stress? These questions shift you from autopilot to awareness.

Another strategy is **curating your feed**. Unfollow accounts that make you feel anxious, inadequate, or irritated. Follow people who educate, uplift, and inspire. Use mute and block functions liberally—they exist to protect your peace. Your feed should reflect your values and goals, not pull you into comparison or conflict.

Also, engage in **active consumption** instead of passive scrolling. Leave thoughtful comments. Save meaningful posts. Share content with purpose. The more intentional your activity, the less vulnerable you are to algorithmic manipulation or emotional fatigue.

Finally, reconnect with **offline activities**. Go for walks without your phone. Journal. Read books. Talk to people face-to-face. Pursue hobbies that don't require screens. These analog moments restore balance, reduce anxiety, and help rewire your attention span.

Remember, a digital detox isn't about rejection—it's about *resetting*. Social media isn't inherently bad. It becomes harmful when it dominates your life, steals your attention, or controls your emotions. Mindful use turns it back into a healthy tool—a way to connect, express, and grow without becoming consumed.

Your time and attention are precious. Protect them with purpose.

Maya's social media detox story

Maya realized something was wrong when she caught herself scrolling through Instagram in the middle of the night—again. It wasn't even a conscious decision. She had woken up to use the bathroom, grabbed her phone out of habit, and before she knew it, she was 45 minutes deep into videos of strangers' vacations, beauty tutorials, and inspirational quotes that all started to blur together.

She wasn't enjoying it. She wasn't learning anything. She was just *there*, scrolling.

That morning, Maya felt foggy and disconnected. She'd had this feeling before—groggy mornings, anxious afternoons, nights that disappeared into her phone. She blamed stress, lack of motivation, or even her diet. But as she looked through her screen time report, the truth became impossible to ignore: she was spending almost five hours a day on social media. That was 35 hours a week—more than a full-time job.

She thought about how that time was spent: endlessly watching reels, checking likes, responding to group chats, comparing herself to influencers, and refreshing feeds that never ended. She missed reading books. She missed writing in her journal. She missed real conversations that weren't interrupted by notifications.

So, Maya decided to try something radical: a one-week digital detox.

She didn't delete her accounts, but she removed Instagram, TikTok, and Facebook from her phone. She turned off all non-essential notifications. She set her phone to grayscale and placed it across the room while working. It felt strange at first—like a phantom limb was missing—but by day three, the fog began to lift.

She noticed little things. The quiet of a morning walk. The sound of her own thoughts. How long a minute actually was. She journaled again. She called a friend just to chat. She went to a yoga class without checking her phone afterward. She realized how much time she had been giving away without thinking.

When the detox ended, Maya reinstalled the apps—but this time with rules. No social media before breakfast or after 9 p.m. One scroll session per day, max 30 minutes. She unfollowed every account that made her feel insecure or distracted. She filled her feed with educators, artists, and friends who uplifted her. She even set a Sunday "no scroll" rule—a weekly break to reset.

Maya didn't become anti-technology. She still shared photos, messaged friends, and used social media to promote her work. But now, it was intentional. It didn't own her attention anymore. She was no longer scrolling to escape—she was showing up with clarity.

The change was subtle but powerful. She felt less anxious, more focused, more herself. She laughed more. Slept better. Thought deeper. All because she took back control of something that had quietly taken over her life.

Digital detoxing didn't mean disconnecting forever. It meant reconnecting—with herself.

Chapter 9: Social Media for Professionals

In today's digital-first world, your online presence often serves as your first impression. Whether you're applying for a job, building a business, networking with peers, or freelancing your skills, social media has become a core component of your **professional brand**. But while social platforms offer powerful opportunities to connect and grow, they can also damage your credibility or expose private aspects of your life if not managed wisely.

A professionally managed digital footprint can open doors. A poorly curated one can quietly close them. That's why it's essential to **separate your personal and professional lives online**, control what's publicly visible, and ensure that your social media reflects your values, expertise, and goals—not just your hobbies or emotions.

Start by conducting a **professional audit of your online presence**. Google your full name, along with keywords like your profession or city. Look at your LinkedIn, Facebook, Instagram, and even old accounts you may have forgotten. What comes up? What would a potential employer, client, or collaborator see? Is it aligned with who you are professionally?

Next, make a clear distinction between **personal accounts** and **professional-facing profiles**. Ideally, use different usernames, email addresses, and privacy settings for each. On platforms like LinkedIn, everything should be professional. But on more casual platforms like Instagram or TikTok, consider whether your personal content might negatively impact how you're perceived in your industry. If needed, create a separate "public" account for career content and set your personal one to private.

Be aware that even "private" profiles may be searchable, tagged, or screenshotted. So before posting anything, ask yourself: "Would I be comfortable with a future employer or client seeing this out of context?" If the answer is no, keep it offline.

On **LinkedIn**, make sure your profile is complete, up to date, and clear. Use a professional headshot, write a compelling summary, and list relevant accomplishments. Avoid buzzwords without context—be specific about your achievements. Connect strategically, engage with thought leaders, and share insights that showcase your expertise.

On **Instagram or TikTok**, if you're using them for branding, keep your bio clear and aligned with your niche. Use content pillars (e.g., education, testimonials, behind-the-scenes) to guide your posts. Highlight your experience and voice in a way that's relatable and authentic. But avoid oversharing, commenting impulsively, or posting content that could be interpreted as unprofessional or polarizing.

Be cautious with political, religious, or controversial content, especially on mixed personal/professional accounts. Even if your views are valid, they can unintentionally alienate clients, colleagues, or hiring managers. Know your audience, and remember that nuance rarely survives in digital spaces.

Your **comments and likes** also shape your professional image. People often forget that liking or commenting on inappropriate posts can still reflect poorly on you, even if your own content is clean. Always assume that your activity is being recorded—and judged.

Consider setting up **Google Alerts** for your name or business name. This way, you'll be notified when new content about you appears online. Stay ahead of your reputation by managing it proactively.

Finally, use **privacy tools and visibility settings** to control what parts of your profile are publicly visible. For example, on LinkedIn, you can hide your connections list. On Facebook, you can restrict past posts from being visible to non-friends.

On Instagram, you can archive or close friends-tag sensitive stories.

The ultimate goal is balance: you want to be discoverable, relatable, and authentic—without being vulnerable or careless. When done right, social media becomes a strategic asset in your career toolkit. It allows you to tell your story, attract new opportunities, and connect with a global network—all while maintaining your integrity and peace of mind.

In the modern world, your resume may open a door—but your online presence can decide whether or not it stays open.

Now, I want to talk about Trevor

Trevor was excited. He had just landed an interview for a job he really wanted—communications coordinator for a rising nonprofit. He had the experience, the references, and the enthusiasm. As he prepared for the interview, he brushed up on industry trends, polished his resume, and picked out his best blazer.

But what Trevor didn't know was that before he ever walked into the room, the hiring manager had already Googled him.

At first glance, Trevor's LinkedIn looked great—clear profile photo, impressive job history, active posts. But a few more clicks led to his Twitter feed, where his tone was... less polished. There were late-night rants, sarcastic takes on current events, and jokes that could easily be misinterpreted. On Instagram, his personal account was public and filled with party photos, half-finished workout selfies, and captions that revealed more about his dating life than his professionalism.

None of it was malicious or even offensive. But it didn't paint the picture of someone ready to represent an organization's mission.

Trevor didn't get the job.

Frustrated, he reached out for feedback—and was gently told that "another candidate was a better cultural fit." That night, he took a hard look at his digital presence. For years, he had treated social media as a personal playground, never thinking about how it might affect his career.

So, Trevor began making changes.

He created a professional Instagram account where he shared communication tips, nonprofit storytelling examples, and moments from conferences and workshops he attended. He kept his personal account but made it private and removed anything that felt too revealing or immature. He stopped posting impulsively and started scheduling thoughtful content that aligned with his career goals.

On Twitter, he deleted hundreds of old tweets and started engaging in conversations around media ethics and digital advocacy. He followed thought leaders in his field, retweeted research, and asked insightful questions. His tone matured—not fake, just intentional.

He also revisited his LinkedIn. He updated his profile photo to something more polished, rewrote his headline to reflect his actual expertise, and added volunteer work and certifications that had been missing. He started posting regularly—short updates about projects, lessons learned from job interviews, and reflections on communication trends.

Within two months, a recruiter messaged him on LinkedIn about a new opportunity—one that ended in a successful offer. This time, the hiring team praised his online presence. "We love how you present yourself," the interviewer said. "It really gave us a sense of your professionalism and voice."

Trevor realized that in a digital world, his **online footprint wasn't separate from his career—it *was* part of it.** Every comment, every photo, every bio contributed to how people perceived him, long before they met him in person.

He didn't delete his personality—he just became more aware of how it showed up online. He learned that social media could be a powerful platform for growth, connection, and credibility—*when used with purpose.*

From then on, Trevor made a habit of checking his digital reflection regularly. Because he knew that in today's world, your brand isn't what you say about yourself—it's what others find when they search your name.

Chapter 10: Build a Privacy-First Social Media Strategy

At this stage, you've explored the many ways social media can affect your privacy, mental health, professional image, and even your relationships. The next step is putting all of that knowledge into practice by building your own **privacy-first social media strategy**—a personalized system that allows you to enjoy the benefits of being online without compromising your control, data, or dignity.

The truth is, you don't need to disappear from the internet to protect your privacy. You simply need a strategy that aligns with your values, your goals, and your boundaries. It begins with intentionality. Ask yourself: *Why am I using each platform?* If the answer is unclear or if a platform constantly drains your energy, consider stepping away or deleting it altogether. You don't have to be everywhere.

Once you've narrowed your focus to the platforms that serve you, take time to **rebuild your profiles with privacy in mind**. For personal accounts, use a **minimalist approach**. Include only what's necessary. Remove birthdays, relationship statuses, cities of residence, or workplace details unless absolutely essential. Use a pseudonym or nickname if privacy is a top concern. For profile pictures, avoid using facial photos that can be scanned by facial recognition systems—consider using an avatar, object, or filtered image.

Next, **adjust visibility settings**. Make your posts visible only to friends or custom lists. Disable search engine indexing and restrict who can send friend requests, message you, or tag you in photos. Many platforms allow you to review posts you're tagged in before they go public—activate this setting. Turn off or limit location tracking, story sharing, face recognition, and ad personalization features.

If you use social media for business or public communication, develop a separate "public profile" with curated content that reflects your values and expertise—but excludes sensitive personal details. Consider **using a content calendar** and limiting real-time posting to avoid location-based vulnerabilities. Maintain a professional tone and keep personal matters off your business-facing accounts.

Another key element of a privacy-first strategy is **controlling third-party access**. Many people don't realize how many apps and services they've connected to their social profiles over time—games, quizzes, plugins, shopping apps, and more. These connections often remain active for years and continue collecting your data. Review your "Apps and Websites" or "Connected Apps" sections on each platform and revoke access to anything unnecessary.

To go a step further, adopt **privacy-enhancing tools** such as virtual private networks (VPNs), encrypted messaging apps, anti-tracking browser extensions, and metadata scrubbing tools. Use privacy-focused platforms like Signal for messaging, Brave or Firefox for browsing, and ProtonMail or Tutanota for secure email communication.

Also, consider how **searchable and traceable** your content is. If you want to be less visible, avoid using your full name, geotags, or exact timestamps. Don't overshare about your daily routine, family members, or upcoming travel. Remember: privacy isn't just about what you post—it's about the patterns you create.

In addition to defense, build proactive habits into your strategy. Set a **quarterly privacy checkup** where you review your account settings, delete unnecessary content, update passwords, and evaluate which platforms still serve your goals. Think of it as a digital oil change.

Most importantly, remember that **you control your narrative**. Don't let algorithms, advertisers, or influencers determine what you share, when you share it, or how you feel about yourself. If you want to post less, do it. If you want to unfollow, mute, or block, do it. If you want to disappear for a week or a year, that's your right.

Building a privacy-first social media strategy doesn't mean being paranoid or hiding. It means **choosing to engage from a place of strength** rather than convenience. It means protecting your future by being mindful in the present.

Your privacy is your power. Protect it with purpose—and use your online presence on your terms.

Nina's opt in story

Nina had always loved social media. As a freelance writer and part-time travel blogger, her posts were vibrant, engaging, and filled with personal details. Her followers knew where she was staying, what coffee shop she visited that morning, and what books she was reading. She loved sharing—it made her feel connected. Until one day, things got too personal.

She had just landed in Lisbon when she received a message from a follower: "I saw you at the café near your Airbnb—small world!" Nina was stunned. She hadn't shared her Airbnb name, just a photo of the front door and a tag of the neighborhood. But it had been enough. The realization unsettled her—how easily her posts revealed her exact location, travel schedule, and even habits. She hadn't been hacked or harassed, but something had shifted. The intimacy of her online life had started to feel exposed.

When she returned home, Nina decided it was time to rethink her entire approach.

She didn't want to quit social media—she enjoyed the creativity and the community. But she wanted to feel in control again. She started with a digital cleanup. She removed exact locations from her captions. She archived hundreds of old posts that included street names, friends' tags, or identifiable details. She changed her profile to a nickname and updated her email to a separate alias used only for social media.

Then she went deeper. She reviewed every connected app and revoked permissions she no longer recognized. She downloaded her data archive from Instagram and was shocked at the amount of metadata the platform had stored—locations, device IDs, facial tags, and even deleted messages. It made her rethink the permanence of her digital actions.

She adjusted her settings across platforms. On Instagram, she disabled ad personalization and removed all interests the app had assigned to her. On Facebook, she set her friend list to private, turned off face recognition, and restricted who could find her by phone number. She began using a VPN when browsing and switched to Signal for private conversations. Her default now was "opt out" instead of "opt in."

But the biggest shift was internal. Nina started planning her content ahead of time—posting after she left a location instead of while she was still there. She stopped sharing out of boredom or pressure and started posting with purpose. She no longer felt the need to explain her absences. When she took time off from social media, she didn't apologize for it—she celebrated it.

The transformation wasn't immediate, but it was powerful. Nina felt lighter. Safer. More focused on her real life than her feed. Her audience remained, and they respected her boundaries. In fact, many told her they appreciated her new approach—it inspired them to rethink their own online habits.

Nina learned that you don't have to disappear to be private. You just have to be intentional. Her privacy-first strategy didn't make her less visible—it made her more *authentic.* And in a world that rewards oversharing, choosing what *not* to share became her greatest strength.

Now, every time she opens an app, she pauses and asks, "Is this true to me? Does this need to be public? Will I be proud of this tomorrow?" If the answer is yes, she posts. If not, she lets it go.

Her digital life no longer feels like a performance. It feels like peace.

Take Back Control of Your Online Life

Social media isn't going away. It's woven into the fabric of modern communication, business, politics, education, and self-expression. It connects families across continents, gives voice to the unheard, and brings communities together around shared passions and causes. But as you've now seen, it also poses profound risks to your privacy, security, mental health, and long-term reputation.

This book wasn't meant to scare you away from the digital world—it was written to **empower** you within it.

You've learned how every like, comment, tag, and upload becomes part of your **digital footprint**. You've uncovered how metadata silently records where you've been and what you've done. You've discovered the existence of **shadow profiles**—invisible dossiers that platforms build even if you never sign up. You've seen how **AI and algorithms manipulate emotions**, and how **oversharing can affect kids and teens for life**. And you've walked through practical ways to reduce exposure, detox from screen overload, and reshape your professional presence with intention.

Most importantly, you've learned that **privacy is not about hiding—it's about protecting what matters most**. Your attention, your time, your personal information, and your digital identity all deserve boundaries. You don't owe your life to the internet. You don't have to perform every moment. You don't have to be always available, always perfect, or always visible.

The beauty of privacy is that it gives you the **freedom to be fully yourself**—without needing to package that self into an algorithm-friendly brand. It allows you to speak freely, think deeply, and connect authentically—without fear that your data will be mined, misused, or misunderstood.

It's easy to feel helpless in the face of Big Tech. After all, these platforms have billions of users, teams of engineers, and powerful algorithms that shape global behavior. But you don't need to fight the system to win. All you need to do is **make conscious choices** about how you use it. Where you scroll. What you post. Who you allow into your digital space. What you protect—and what you let go.

Start small. Audit your accounts. Clean up your profiles. Adjust your settings. Log out more often. Limit what you share—and delay what you post. Practice mindful engagement instead of impulsive reaction. Step away from your feed when it starts to feel more like a burden than a benefit. Teach your children to value their privacy early. And help your friends do the same.

Remember that your **digital footprint is a living thing**. It changes with every post, photo, and interaction. That means it can also be *redirected*, *refined*, and *reclaimed*. You are not stuck with the choices of your past. You are not trapped in someone else's algorithm. You are not just a user—you are a *participant*, and participants have power.

Your journey doesn't end here. In fact, it's just beginning. Every day, you'll face decisions about what to share, what to protect, and how to engage with the world around you. With the right knowledge and mindset, you can turn social media into a tool for **growth, connection, and creativity**—without sacrificing your freedom, privacy, or peace of mind.

You don't need to be a cybersecurity expert to make better digital decisions. You just need awareness. And now you have that.

So take what you've learned, share it with others, and start showing up online the way you *choose*—not the way the system expects.

Because in the end, the most powerful thing you can do is simple: **Own your presence. Protect your privacy. And never forget—you are in control.**

www.ingramcontent.com/pod-product-compliance
Lightning Source LLC
LaVergne TN
LVHW022023200926
848481LV00007B/2514

* 9 7 9 8 3 4 9 6 4 5 1 5 0 *